Magnificat

Magnificat

Poems by Marilyn Nelson Waniek

Louisiana State University Press

Baton Rouge and London

1994

Designer: *Glynnis Phoebe*
Typeface: *text Granjon, display Antique Solid*
Typesetter: *G & S Typesetters, Inc.*
Printer and binder: *Thomson-Shore, Inc.*

Library of Congress Cataloging-in-Publication Data
Waniek, Marilyn Nelson, 1946–
    Magnificat : poems / by Marilyn Nelson Waniek.
    p.   cm.
    ISBN 0-8071-1921-0 (cloth). — ISBN 0-8071-1922-9 (paper)
    I. Title.
PS3573.A4795M29   1994
811'.54—dc20   94-6066
                                                        CIP

"Dusting," "Tell Me a Story," and "Enigma Variations" first ap-
peared in *Ploughshares.* "Renunciation," "Psalms," and "Matins"
first appeared in *Kenyon Review.* "Abba Jacob and the Angel,"
"Solitude as Soweto," and "Abba Jacob at Bat" first appeared in
Southern Review. "The Sacrament of Poverty" and "Epithala-
mium and Shivaree" first appeared in *Obsidian II.* "The Ploti-
nus Suite" first appeared in *New Virginia Review.* "A Canticle
for Abba Jacob" first appeared in *A Formal Feeling Comes:
Poems in Form by Contemporary Women,* edited by Annie Finch
(Story Line Press). "Palm Psalm" first appeared in the Philoma-
thean Society Anthology honoring Daniel Hoffman, edited by
Sonny Bosco (Princeton University Press). "Abba Jacob and
St. Francis" first appeared in *Poems for a Small Planet: Contem-
porary American Nature Poetry,* edited by Robert Pack and Jay
Parini (University Press of New England). The author grate-
fully acknowledges the editors of these publications.

Title page illustration: Drawing by Henri Cartier-Bresson
based on *Jacob Wrestling with the Angel,* by Delacroix. Courtesy
Henri Cartier-Bresson. Used with permission.

Everything is gratuitous, everything is gift.
— *David Steindl-Rast, O.S.B.*

My gratitude is due many people who assisted me with this project. Several are Benedictine monks who, I imagine, would not wish their names mentioned. I will, however, thank by name Gunilla Norris; Tom Jambeck; Rev. Julia Gatta; Bill Curtin; Bill Larkin, C.S.P.; Rev. John Moren; Rev. Mother Mary Peter, O.S.B.; Bill Cain, S.J.; Rev. Phil Rider; Rev. Bennett Brockman; and George Winchester, S.J. Thanks to the Benedictine monks of Weston Priory, and to Las Misioneras Guadalupanas de Cristo Rey, O.S.B. Thanks to my ace boon friend, Pamela Espeland, for moral support. Thanks to Dave Ganoe for the loons.

My gratitude, too, to the National Endowment for the Arts, the Connecticut Commission for the Arts, and the University of Connecticut Research Foundation for fellowships or grants that freed me to pursue my project.

To my husband, St. Roger B. Wilkenfeld

Contents

IV   Ordinary Time

I

Lost and Found

Letter to a Benedictine Monk

Dear Frère Jacques,
Every night a new loneliness:
So much love for the lost.
And once or twice a month for more than twenty years
I've dreamed of a lost boy
and waked an unnameable ache.

When we met at a party
morning bells rang
at first sight.
He kissed my hand,
looked into my eyes,
said he'd never cease
loving me.
His white shirt and pants,
the sunkissed wave
curving over his brow:
I answered his open gaze
with an equal promise.

I prowled past his house many midnights
like a cat in season.
We seemed to be friends:
We both wrote poems;
we waved on campus;
sometimes we talked:
whenever we met
that same silver tingle
rang in my chest.

Once, he asked me out.
We drove in circles for hours, lost
on the way to a drive-in,
confused by the road map,
the roads, and the warmth
a few inches away.

We drove home in silence.
"Don't say anything," he said;
"Don't get up."
He left me posed,
a black madonna,
on my living room floor.
I'd waited two years
for the kiss he withheld.

One summer evening
just after we graduated,
some of my friends came over
for wine and cheese.
We were moving, taking off
for what we called Real Life.
This was his last American night.
He was staying with someone
whose name I didn't catch.
Nonchalant as you please
on the floor in front of the couch,
knowing I'd die
if I didn't touch him,
my heart stopped as stone in my mouth,
as everyone got up to go
I placed one hand
on his foot.

The last guest to leave,
he turned in my doorway:
"Will you sleep with me?"

My laughter.
I've been waiting for you
all this time,
and now it's impossible,
it's too late,
at last,
yes:
it meant. And the boy ran
to his motorbike and roared
into the road before I stopped
laughing.

I ran after, crying his name,
but *ex machina* a freight train
muted my voice.
He didn't look back.

Frère Jacques,
I think of you often,
and pray you are happy and well.
What a search it has been.
Forgive me. I loved him.
But perhaps you don't
remember me at all.

Compline

The evening is as quiet
as a monk at prayer.
The children asleep,
the TV steel-green;
the Christmas tree cradles
fifty electric candles.
Stretched out on the couch
I at last close my eyes.

And immediately
fall asleep.
Despite miles of highways
paved with good intentions.
The car feels safe,
there's a whole tank of gas,
only one or two headlights grow
in my windshield and mirror.

Where am I going?
Can you tell me,
my dear

friend?
Because damned if I know.
The miles-per-hour landscape
offers a million illegible exits.
Was the one I sped past
twenty years ago
the right way?
The one I passed
today?

I wake with a start:
no answers.
I turn off the tree,
nudge the toys into a corner,
and tiptoe from
bedroom to bedroom
to bedroom. It is good
to give thanks.

Lost and Found

I

The crystal wind-chimes in the evening rain,
the faint stir of the wind soughing the leaves,
the loon's
despairing, god-hungry banshee
laughter, almost human.
The moonlit lake bordered by white trunks.
The tidy garden rows.
The gladsome noise
told by a bell. The quietly assembling monks.

The half-risen from sleep,
their stiff fingers wiping tear-bleary eyes.
The silence of these men who keep
the scattered coals of faith alive,
who breathe them into fire.
Their fifteen bare and lowered heads—
tousled, still, from lonely beds.
Their shadows' candlelit dance as they join in prayer.

Lover by lover, they renounce our world.
Do they feel as we feel?
Rejoice at mail?
Do their eyes remain narrow sometimes for days?
At what cost do they will to will their peace?
How do they know they're called?
How achingly I long to be the friend
of such a man. My tenderness is real:
He has remained for years a raw, unhealed
rent in my conscience. Yet by offering
my spirit's touch
perhaps I've set him ten years back.
Maybe I'm sick,
my love profane or a perversion:
Am I just turned on by vocations?
He prays in solitude.
I write, knowing my letters lie unread.

May he be touched? I just want to touch him
lightly as angel-down. To love
someone who's looked from the far summit of
fathomless yearning. Just to touch
a man whose sole desire is to detach
himself from self and secret sin,
who wills his lifetime to become
a great zero, filled with the purest prayer.
I write to say I hold him dear,
to call him by his truest name.
By doing so,
I'm asking him to break a vow,
without even hoping to glimpse his face.

Embrace, erase, embrace, erase, embrace
runs our implicit dialogue—
one side of it unspoken.
But one side deafening. For I have broken
his silence with my pilgrimage,
aroused his pride with hero-worship,
made him remember, perhaps,
a girl who stopped laughing too late.
Perhaps he hears her now, from the dark lake.

II

I push aside the stone, wince at the light.
Who calls me to this labor of rebirth:
desire which nothing can requite?
Halfway around the earth,
a man who prays.
And I'm amazed:
I read him loud and clear
over the static of despair.
How a woman must work, loving a priest,
to lead him not into temptation
(although it *is* a part of life . . .).
And convinced I am the least
worthy to walk into his contemplation
when he may be on the verge of knowing Christ,
I swoon, blinded by dazzle:

8

What a razzmatazz!
I'll always love this man.
I want to be his friend.
But everything I do is wrong, is wrong.
But everything I am is wrong.

Am I the child of Sarah, or of Eve,
I wonder at the mailbox, as I drop
another envelope into his lap.
Can it be fair to him
to send in letters blotched by tears
passion I've saved up for twenty years
since he raced off? I make believe
he reads them less as lovesongs than as hymns.

I cannot live with him, yet this is life:
sudden and unchanged, and paradise.
I see the ordinary through his eyes;
I get good news by psychic telegraph.
He's a pair of 3-D glasses just my size:
now I have perfect, plenty/plenty vision.
I've found him, and I gush with gratitude,
a wondering exile stumbling into Zion.
Et cetera. Dare I go on?
I love his God, though, not the man,
I argue like a politician.
He held the door;
what was I waiting for?
I spend an hour each day knocking on wood.
He struggles to be pure,
to live in poverty,
to love unselfishly;
he offers up his life as an oblation.
My letters knock, rush in, shout "me, me, me!"
rattling the walls of his serenity.
How do I love him? Count infinity.
He loves me for Christ's sake:
I'm unkissed, and awake.

But should I leave his desert to its peace?
Forget his saying that he'd never cease
loving me, the first instant our eyes met?

For years I've borne the weight of this regret;
I know another straw would break my heart.
I'd die before I'd hurt this man again.
But he might need a friend
to help him celebrate,
to be his telephone into the world.
How will I prove I'm not a silly girl
mooning over a tale of lost true love?
What can I offer him? What do I have
a monk might use? In all my everything,
for all my searching, I can't find a thing.
I tell him what the children say at play,
what I've been reading, what I pray.
And I ponder:
Frankly, I cannot see
what he would learn from me
but mundane wonder.

Writing by candlelight,
I argue with myself:
Should I admit I'm twenty years too late,
and leave him over there beyond the shelf?
Or catch him in his wilderness,
wrestle him down, ask to be blessed?
Which would be hard-, and which pure-heartedness?
I can't hear anything above the noise
of wind and earthquake. There's no still, small voice.
Help me to make this choice.
Choose for his sake.
—A loon, out on the lake;
it startled me.
Should I renounce him, let him be?
No more invade his sacristy,
unblessing his whole life
with the insistent touch of female hands?
A monk wooed by a wife . . .
(Well, why don't you just *make* him understand!)

Don't we get a happily ever after?
A chance for some shared laughter?
I could love God through him;
he could love God through me:

Thus runs the best of many arguments,
of which none seems particularly heaven-sent.
Please help me. *Choose for his sake.*
—A loon. Wind on the lake.
Which should I hope:
That he can take the leap
and trust me, or that somehow I can keep
from calling like a pilgrim at his cave,
and leave him to his dialogue?
For his sake. —A railroad whistle in the fog.
For his sake, in the name of love,
I bow to silence. And herewith I leave
a kiss of blessing on his brow.
Thus, I renounce a world: I share his vow.

III

You will forever be a mystery,
my . . . My friend.
This letter marks the end
of my best hope. (But then again, maybe . . .)
I'd gilded you with halo paint,
lost my last shred of self-restraint.
I wanted you to be a saint.
You would have been my private miracle:
a base for faith, in the empirical.
I wanted you to recognize
my lovesongs as a hymn of praise.
I hoped you'd echo my desire
to stand up naked, soul to soul,
in one flash changing nothingness to fire.
Forgive my loss of self-control.
I'd hoped to share the wait for death.
I'd hoped you'd wait with me for death.

A psalmody of loons sings the dark blues
of how I feel.
I've found you. And it hurts like hell.
All the love we'll never use.
The courage we can't dare,
the hope we'll never share,

but warehouse in the heart's midwest
behind a padlocked iron door.
Yet from your silent gesture I can guess
the jubilation you must pray.
For giving everything away
increases everything, so we are fed
a miracle of fish and bread.
As silence falls between us once again,
I know that I've been blessed:
My miracle the hard gift of the pain
of finding you, to give you up for lost.

II

Plain Songs

Incomplete Renunciation

Please let me have
a 10-room house adjacent to campus;
6 bdrooms, 2½ baths, formal
dining room, frplace, family room,
screened porch, 2-car garage.
Well maintained.
And let it pass
through the eye of a needle.

Prayer on the Wing

Wow. I don't have time right now
to offer a decent prayer.
Thanks for everything.
And could you extend
a sort of blanket
blessing?

Psalm

So many cars have driven past me
without a head-on collision.
I started counting them today:
there were a hundred and nine
on the way to the grocery,
a hundred and two on the way back home.
I got my license
when I was seventeen.
I've driven across country
at least twelve times;
I even drive
late Saturday nights.
I shall not want.

Tell Me a Story

Back in the drafty hovel,
the fishwife nonetheless
wants.
My daughter pats my cheek,
asks what I want.
Too much, I sigh:
the moment already lost
in her childhood past.

The Dream's Wisdom

I dreamed
Mama came back
for a borrowed day.
We knew she would die again;
her heart was irrevocably set.
She was so dear to me.
I knew
a new
gentleness.

Help me greet everyone I know
with the dream's
wisdom.

Matins (2:30 A.M.)

One-third of the world
is dreaming right now of food.
Another third stares
into empty handmade bowls,
and I can't sleep
for indigestion.

Is this pain heartburn,
or the autopsy's reason
for my incomprehensible death?
They die
anonymous:
Sudanese children.
Lebanese mother
holding her limp, long baby.
Decimated villagers.

They cry,
What can I have done
to deserve this pain?
This soul-killing fear?

And my meshuggenah fear.
That so many should hunger while I promise
never again to Really Eat The Whole Thing;
that they should sleep in the open wind
while I hope for posthumous anthology fame;
that they should need
while I lie wondering
how long it will take my husband
to drive me to the emergency room,
and how to spell relief.
Jesus. I must be the smallest grain
of the salt of the earth.

Dusting

Thank you for these tiny
particles of ocean salt,
pearl-necklace viruses,
winged protozoans:
for the infinite,
intricate shapes
of sub-microscopic
living things.

For algae spores
and fungus spores,
bonded by vital
mutual genetic cooperation,
spreading their
inseparable lives
from equator to pole.

My hand, my arm,
make sweeping circles.
Dust climbs the ladder of light.
For this infernal, endless chore,
for these eternal seeds of rain:
Thank you. For dust.

Enigma Variations

Elgar, Enigma Variations, *Op. 36*

For what
does my longing long?

Exactly how
infinite are you?

Who's
going to die?

Military
intelligence.

(Military intelligence?
Is that what I said?)

In laughter hope
meets despair.

Play it for me, Sam.
At my funeral.

Gloria

I praise your name, Lord,
for postal efficiency.
By your gracious hand
mail is forwarded
to the correct local address.
I praise you,
Lord of surprise and elation,
for a telegraph message
of nine perfect words.

Who could doubt your mercy,
opening the mailbox
so hopelessly,
and then laughing with tears
in the spring-bearing wind?
Or doubt your grace,
holding one blue,
long-awaited
fluttering wing?

I will sing unto the Lord,
for what was lost
has been found again.
My thin voice rises
on the air of this,
one of the best blest days
you have ever made.

Palm Psalm

A three-stringed lyre
covered with cobwebs.
A going-nowhere roadmap
with a trapezoid bull's-eye.
My love-line,
my line of influence,
the end of my life.
Oh magnify the Lord.

The Prayer of Silence

I've fought off the octopi and the Great White Shark,
and drifted into silence:
On the far wall a glass-brick cross
filters early morning light.
A veteran candle on the low altar,
a jar of dried grasses,
a painted cross on an easel,
a sad-eyed ikon
of a woman
holding a baby.
High on the right wall
a plain wooden cross.
A man on a wicker stool,
his head bowed,
his hands folded.

He stands, opens his arms,
looks up, closes his eyes,
and takes in
radiance.

III

A Desert Father

The Fruit of Faith

Abba Jacob, on the word
of his master,
planted a walking stick
and watered it every day
for seven years.
In the seventh year it grew leaves.
In the eighth it produced
a wholly new fruit.

Come,
says the master.
Partake.

Abba Jacob and Miracles

One day Abba Jacob
was praying in a sunbeam
by the door to his underground cell,
and the brethren came to him
to ask him about miracles.
One of the elders said,
My mother's spirit came back
and turned out all the lights
the night we gathered for her wake:
Was that a miracle?
Another said, One spring evening
a white rainbow of mist
passed over our heads:
Was that a miracle?
They went on like this
for several hours.
Abba Jacob listened.
Then there was silence.

Big deal,
said Abba Jacob.
Miracles happen all the time.
We're here,
aren't we?

Abba Jacob's Aside on Hell

Abba Jacob said:
I wonder if souls are unhappy
in hell.
I rather doubt it.
And if they are
they won't admit it,
like people in an expensive nightclub,
glad-handed by the rich and beautiful,
while the rich
and the beautiful
hold cold hands
to a fire in a dustbin.

Abba Jacob and the Theologian

Thanking him for spending
the entire afternoon
and half the dinner hour
discussing the various ramifications
of the essentially paradoxical nature
of faith,
the theologian interrupts her first
spoonful of lentils
to lean forward again
and cut off
the flow of God.
Reverend Father, she asks,
what is the highest spiritual virtue?

Abba Jacob looks to heaven
and groans.
Humor, he says.
Not seriously, of course.

Abba Jacob and the Businessman

A businessman heard about Abba Jacob
and went to see him
about his difficulties
with mental prayer.
Abba Jacob
was planting trees.
When the businessman saw him
he said, Boy,
tell me where the cell
of Abba Jacob is.
Abba Jacob said:
What do you want with him?
The man is a fool.

Oh, said the businessman,
turning away.
I heard he
was holy.

Abba Jacob and St. Francis

Abba Jacob with his invention—
a flashlight lantern on a cord around his neck—
balances tiptoe on an upended barrel.
There's one,
he mutters, and reaches.
The damned creatures
are making lace
of my arbor.
He holds each beetle for a moment,
then breaks it and tosses it aside.
The watching guests,
laughing, tease him:
So much for St. Francis.

Abba Jacob says:
Well, at least I don't call them
brother
and *then* kill them.

But I do
ask God's pardon.

Purgatory

Abba Jacob said:
A friend came to me with a problem.
It seemed he'd smiled at a tramp
and wound up asking the man
to come home and live in the garage.
He and his wife agreed
it was the only thing to do.
For the first three days
everything went swimmingly.
On the fourth morning
of hair in the sink,
the toilet unflushed,
the towels crooked,
the soap dirty and wet,
his wife threw a tantrum.
For several weeks
they'd been living in hell,
torn between caring for the poor
and packing him off.

I told him to throw the bum out,
said Abba Jacob.
That tramp
was not poor.
I'll probably spend time
in Purgatory for that.

Abba Jacob's Seven Devils

Another miracle
comes knocking at his door,
crying Father.
Another penitent,
another seeker,
another love.
He puts her up
in the guesthouse
and calls it
The Queen's Palace.
The last sleeper in its bed
a worn hooker
he found in the street.
She says he's a saint,
too.
      All night the dogs howl.

Abba Jacob and the Angel

homage to Henri Cartier-Bresson

In the end Abba Jacob gave up
trying to wrestle with the angel.
She was stronger than he,
and a full head
wiser.
He panted
against her shoulder
as she took his hand in hers
and put her arm around his neck.
Then he heard the music.

Free Lunch

All this gratuitous beauty:
azure and aquamarine.
A black dog and a brown
nuzzle my fingers
when we meet on the beach.
All this scot-free grace.
A drop of spilled juice
trembles on the table.
I bow to its sweetness,
drink.

Hog Heaven

With a serious, clerical look
a skinny hen pecks lice
off the belly of a smiling pig.
Sometimes the best thanksgiving
is a grunt of pure peace.

Abba Jacob and the Muse

Museum of the Absurd.
In every room the odd,
the untoward, the eccentric,
Abba Jacob wrote one night.
Ridiculous mind. A gecko heard
him laughing to himself. *Clod-*
hopper, circus sad-face. Your one trick
juggling pebbles on a derelict site.

Solitude as Soweto

I seek you in narrow sleep;
still you are hidden.
Awake, your name a pendulum
from pulse to pulse
through the whir in my ears,
I listen. And you keep silence.
Feel how unfolding petal by petal
emptiness waits for you:
My heart a cardboard shanty
where five grown men
weep toward dawn.

The Bread of Desire

Fancy cracker in a silver monstrance,
host of love's banquet,
I kneel before you in my cell.
All the wild horses
of rational thought
froth against faith.
Dawn, mid-morning,
afternoon, dusk
a Sahara of longing.
Then suddenly I
become nothing: You
      are.
The world balanced
on impossible truth.

Abba Jacob at Bat

A young visitor
wearing an Angels cap
sat down cross-legged
at Abba Jacob's feet.
Abba Jacob said:
That baseball cap
reminds me of the man who died in my arms
when I was twenty-three.
His last words were
Put out the light.

Why baseball caps?
Abba Jacob rose and took his guest's cap,
snapped it twice against his forearm,
put it on and straightened the peak.
He said: Because they remind us
to live.

Abba Jacob Gets Down

Abba Jacob said:
There was once a Desert Father
who had a bad novice.
One day the novice died
and went to hell.
That night the abba
went into ecstasy:
He had a vision of his novice
surrounded by fire.
My son, he said, I pity you
for being there.

That's all right, Father,
the novice replied.
I'm sitting
on three bishops.

A Canticle for Abba Jacob

1

How beautiful you are, my love,
how beautiful you are. I always knew
you were a redwood in a grove
of mangos: shadows under you
fragranced, cool as an Easter morning's dew.

2

Twelve thousand miles. He sees me first,
and calls me. And his eyes are just the same.
I don't know which of these is worse:
the joy of turning toward my name,
or the pain of smothering a rising flame.

3

He talks about a helpless God;
walking with me, he holds up his white hem.
He listens, smiles, and nods. The God
of the Desert Father's apothegms,
who seeks the poor, who lights the world through them.

4

At lunch in the refectory
he feeds me from a papaya with his spoon.
Joy curves in a trajectory
which I visualize as a cartoon
of a contrail fading miles beyond the moon.

5

A paring knife slices my thumb.
He jumps up, takes the bandage from my hand,
and binds it. I feel, yielding, dumb,
his tenderness and his command.
His dark hair . . . We step back. We understand.

6

The territory-marking calls
of morning birds divide darkness from day.
Within white oratory walls
a hermit and a mother pray.
They pray in silence. God knows what they say.

7

Ad te clamamus exsules . . .
How perfectly plainsong's twin poles combine
to raise the soul's lamenting praise,
its joyous heartbreak.
                    I incline
my head and chant: Beloved, I am thine.

8

My Love is coming toward my room.
Like Cinderella on her wedding night,
who waits, breathing her own perfume,
I tremble, heartsick with delight.
The Bridegroom comes. His gentle eyes. His might.

9

I sleep, but my night-watching heart
hears my Beloved calling through the door.
I run to force steel bars apart
and open to Him. But before
I breathe free air He's not there anymore.

10

I seek Him on my bed whom my
heart loves. Impossible. I cannot find
a trace under the curving sky.
And still I cannot stop my mind
searching for Him who left my heart behind.

11

How beautiful You are, my Love,
how beautiful You are.
                    Your changeful eyes,
the humble grace with which you move
your hands, your laughter, your surprise.
Your listening silences. Your God, who dies.

12

He nestles me in His embrace.
Don't rouse my Love. My breath mingles with His.

The quiet contours of his face:
Touch them as I would. I pray this.
Touch him for me, my Lord.
                    My Love! Thy kiss!

Lovesong

after Rilke

How shall I hold my spirit, that it not
touch yours? How shall I send it soaring past
your height into the patient waiting, there
above you? Oh, if only I could shut
it up, leave it to gather velvet dust
someplace where it would echo you no more.
But, like two strings vibrating as the bow
ripples them with a long, caressing stroke,
we tremble, drawn together by one joy.
What instrument is this? Whose fingers make
a chord beyond our capacity for awe?
How sweet, how: *Ah!*

Everyday Holiness

Let's have a quarrel
like other people do,
said Amma Mama.
Abba Jacob said:
All right, I'll try
if you like.
That roll of film you ruined
when you opened my camera . . .

. . . well, it turned out
to be a blessing in disguise.
The only shot left that they could print
was the only one I really cared about.
And look:
Now there's a rainbow!

IV

Ordinary Time

The War of the Heart

*Abba Pambo said, "After a monk has fought all of the other wars,
there still remains the war of the heart."*

The Snows of Kilimanjaro we planted
near the refectory door is blooming.
And last night's shouting match,
which made me close my eyes and count to ten,
broke this morning in a shared smile over the hubbub.
I knock wood for our good health,
our leak-proofed roof, our surfeit of plenty.
Our shoulders almost touched as we walked,
his hands at his back and mine in my skirt pockets,
both of us laughing.

I bounce from love to love in a cloud of wonder:
Jake's deepening giggle, the curve of Dora's eyebrows.
Impossible Roger, more my husband every day. I say,
I'll be with you in a minute, then peek
into memory like a thief with a pouch of hidden jewels.
I close my eyes and call across brown veldt distance,
with an alligator puppet on my hand whom Dora is telling
the story of the ugly duckling. Knowing
I must not long for him. I must not write.
He said, The joy we feel is just a little taste!

Meanwhile he speaks in answering silence.
He sits for a long time without moving during vespers,
then looks up at the ikon and sings the Salve Regina.
He said, In the greatest love, the lovers reach
together toward God. He said, Love is simple.
He said he always seemed to step in dogshit
just before he got to my door; he used to come in,
and toss his shoes out the window before he said hello.
He said, I'll sing a Gloria, because in making you, God
seems for once to have done something pretty well.

So is love a harmonic conjunction of ionized hormones,
or a gesture which creates that toward which it points?
Or a spontaneous decision to believe, made looking
at the joy-star in somebody's eyes?

I hesitated a moment when we met, then leapt
beyond doubt. And look what faith got me:
A weird, almost non-relationship
with an inscrutable, cantankerous old hermit.
Who writes, My deep friendship extends
to everyone you love.

Payday Evening at My Desk

for Mariano Cirilo

Just four solicitations today, and none
with a guilt-inducing "our gift for you,"
pump-priming cash, or undiscardable stamps.
That's almost a record. At this rate, soon
the earth's individual wretched will queue
to our door daily, from their squalid camps
near and far all over the world. Poor, meet
our three mortgages.
                              By early evening light
Señora Carmelita's grandson falls
asleep in his lean-to next to her one-
room tinroof cinderblock home. She and the girls
share her bed. Perhaps their mother will come
back someday with dollars.
                                     The first to guess
how love makes us poor is the IRS.

The Sacrament of Poverty

for Judy Maines

All the children on this ward are dying of AIDS.
The sister opens the door to two hundred and ten
quiet cribs lined in such tight ranks
you can barely squeeze between. This is not
an unpaid advertisement: You left your family,
the local value of your surname, your wind-tight house,
electricity, the safe water we turn on and drink
and went for two weeks to Haiti,
to hold out your arms from a rocking-chair.
One by one babies were handed to you,
their skin smooth as black milk.
Gradually they remembered touch,
met your gaze, surrendered smiles.
One tottered through three wards to find you again;
he stood beside your chair, his cheek pressed to your arm.
All you can do, you said later, *is hold them
and love them. And let them go.*

And now this grief, Judy.
Each day another square to ex through.
You said you were helpless, dumb,
humbled by their pure poverty.
I never even started
your wedding poem.

Valentine for a Bride Bereaved

for Judy

One foot
in front of the other.
One foot
in front of the other
you will cross humpfrozen meadowgrass
to the dappled heart of the wood
where despite your wounded eyes
for a full moment
you will know him with you, waving a wide circle,
his dear voice wondering
why even love can't make us see
all these invisible rainbows.

Epithalamium and Shivaree

for Linda and Debbie

All Cana was abuzz next day with stories:
Some said it had a sad aftertaste; some said
its sweetness made them ache with thirst.
Years later those who had been there
spoke of it with closed eyes, and swayed
like the last slow-dance of the prom.
The village children poked each other's ribs
when they reeled past, still drunk at eighty.

Lovers know what that drunkenness is:
It makes a festive sacrament of praise
for the One who loans us each other
and this too-brief time.
One sip of the wine of Cana
and lovers become fools. And fools lovers.
The willows are drunk tralala; they shimmy
in the silly wind of Spring,

lovers sing noisily. With a little pink parasol
a lover pedals out to the halfway point on the wire.
Below, a silver thread of river. She waves, blows kisses,
wavers, and oops,
her unicycle disappears into mystery.
Her face mimes our gasp.
We hear an unseen slide-whistle chorus.
She sings: *Tralala, the willows are drunk;*

they shimmy in the silly April wind.
And I'm just a kitten in catnip, a pup
rollin' in some ambrosial doggie cologne.
Why settle for less than rapture?
Your pulse against my lips, your solitude
snoring next to mine. The wine we drink from each other.
She leaps. And now there are two of them out there,
jitterbugging on shimmering air.

The Plotinus Suite

I   No Jazz

Hard sex. The silken, honeyed twang of parting.
No effing jazz. A violin, a tad too white.
Rough sex. More sex.
                    Okay, then: Radio silence.
Silence, longing. Never his scent
in my nostrils, his tongue
tasting mine, his smooth . . . Ah, it comes:

Those to whom heaven-passion
is unknown may only guess at it
by the passions of the earth.

Abba Jacob watched a porn film for a few minutes once,
in a monastery on midnight TV. It was sad, he said;
they looked so lonely.

II   Behind a Descartes Bumpersticker

. . . therefore I am? That's not it either.
I love? Could be. A slightly pregnant pause.
How love? And whom? Your faces file in,

quietly take seats, listen. My hoping eyes
scour the horizon. Where is he
whom my essence it is to love?

Our true beloved is elsewhere.
Abba J says there's a little door in the heart
behind which he is hidden.

Even if it bears someone's name,
on a whiff through the keyhole
catch the faint spring fragrance of longing . . .

III To San Francisco

Trunks clunk together behind me and Dora,
full of books, letters, seashells, pottery, stones,
memories, lies I tell myself: A future tag-sale.

Jake and Roger walk, talking scores.
Spare us that debate in the desert
of what stays, what goes. Spare me

the haunted clarity of the survivor
wading down from the thawing pass.
I am dust. I leave a trail of offerings.

Take this, this. My glittering illusions,
my ambition, my pride, but not . . .

Take away everything.

IV The Jesus Prayer

You ought not to ask,
but to understand
in silence.

Have mercy compels each cricket,
each pell-mell thought, the cosmos known
and imagined, to circle in yearning.

If I could go all the way,
beyond sobbing hunger, what might I hear?
Why can't I shut up

that treeful of grackles,
the newsreels and coming attractions,
the camcorder clicking in memories, and just be still?

V Prayer of Singing Joy

Tides of the mantra shore against your silence,
but a little flick of the cortex, and I'm just
pretending to pray.

I pinch off the pink buds
of explicitly sexual fantasy,
take twenty deep breaths,

and when I've finished singing in the east-lit fields,
walk back toward the tiny oratory.
He's still standing there,

his arms outspread.
Caught up, poised in the void,
he has attained to quiet.

VI Hermitage Breakfast

For that hour he is enkindled.
I tiptoe past, put on water for tea,
set the table for two.

He comes in radiant
as a morning-after bridegroom.
Some things one need not ask.

He blesses the table; we sit
to yesterday's tough bread,
steam rising from two cups.

Once in a while he looks at me and smiles.
I know: It was winged light;
it was love's incandescent center.

VII Sneak Preview

The door burst open into a cathedral
filled with   loving light.
Beyond arched windows

in far deep   interior space,
for one fibrillation of a wave of electromagnetic radiation
I was there, extinguished.

I awakened out of the body to myself.
Then I was at my desk,
murmuring, "Oh. I see."

It's just like everyone
says. There's a big

                    light

VIII The True Magic

I had all but one of the family pictures
needed to divide the sections in my last book,
but I couldn't find one of my dad as a Tuskegee cadet.

Two days before the publisher's deadline, my cousin called
to say something weird had happened to him the night before.
He'd gone to his first meeting of Tuskegee Airmen, Inc.

The stranger sitting beside him had asked his connection
to the original group, and Roy had told him Daddy's name.
Oh, said the man; then I guess this must be for you.

Daddy's eyes are looking straight into the camera.
The true magic is the love contained within the universe.
This is the original enchanter.

IX Parable of the Moth

A heliotropic moth looked up
from the screen one June moon evening,
and fell into impossible longing.

He couldn't eat, couldn't sleep.
Blear-eyed on the third noon
he looked up again, into the sun.

His first experience was loving
a great luminary
by means of some thin gleam from it.

Hallowed be, he proclaimed,
and fell into a stupor.
That night he was back at the screen.

X Ennead I. vi.

How do we get to that promised motherland?
What star should we follow?
You can't get there on foot;

your feet only carry you everywhere
in this world, from country to country.
You can't get there by land, sea, or air.

Shut up, close your eyes,
and wake to a new way of seeing.
Go into yourself, look around.

And if what you see there isn't beautiful,
don't stop smoothing, polishing, cutting away until
you are *wholly yourself, nothing but pure light.*

XI Union Apprehended

As facing mirrors clarify each other,
reflecting only light, the shared glance
of those made poor by love reflects union.

What is union?
This penlight I aim into the afternoon:
Where is its beam? It is in union.

Or again: thunder. Lightning casts white nets.
At what point does the sky become the pond?
They are not two. They are union.

Your breath, the universe:
Where does one end and the other begin?
Close your eyes. *Ascend into yourself.*

XII Icarus Dream

Our Jake at three woke up one morning
asking to be dressed so he could go out
and fly. Wide-armed, he ran in circles

for a minute or two; when he came back in,
he no longer believed. Some of us given wings
fly straight to the center of radiant welcome.

An inner, inexorable magnetic north shows the way,
through rings of silence, from solitude
to solitude. The horizon of infinite mystery

is reached in stillness, through an open heart.
If love is a key, I give you mine for Abba Jacob.
Here: Make *the flight of the alone to the Alone.*